Where to eat in DERBYSHIRE & THE PEAK DISTRICT

THE INFORMATIVE GUIDE TO EATING OUT IN DERBYSHIRE

Editor: Jeff Evans
Art and Design: Simon Baker, Michelle Power
Administration: Lisa Rosier
Compilation: Wendy Tapping

CONTENTS

Cover Photograph: Guido's Restaurant-Bar, Derby
Tastes of Derbyshire by Sue Morgan

Published by Kingsclere Publications Ltd.
Highfield House, 2 Highfield Avenue,
Newbury, Berkshire, RG14 5DS

Typeset by Microset Graphics Ltd., Basingstoke, Hampshire

Produced through MRM Associates Ltd., Reading, Berkshire

Distributed in the UK by AA Publishing,
The Automobile Association,
Fanum House, Basingstoke, Hampshire, RG21 2EA

Extreme care is taken to ensure the accuracy of entries, but
neither the Editor nor the Publishers accept any liability
for errors, omissions or other mistakes, or any
consequences arising therefrom.

Foreword

Peter, Tessa and Andrew Bramley

BY ANDREW BRAMLEY

Years ago, the visitor to Derbyshire would have seen a very different culinary picture to the one he sees today. It is thanks to a more discerning public that restaurateurs have improved their standards to meet people's expectations.

Nowadays, it is thankful that many more people use restaurants as an everyday service, as they would the theatre, the cinema, the golf course, the hairdresser, and so on. Look in any European provincial town, and you would see the local restaurants being supported by locals of all walks of life – whether that establishment is a simple rural inn or a grand, world-renowned institution. The common factor is an appreciation of good food.

Several years ago, the same could not be said of provincial England, but times change, and, county by county, standards have improved dramatically. Now Derbyshire is no exception, offering good food right across the board, from country pubs, to bistros and ethnic restaurants, and one or two top-flight restaurants worthy of national praise.

Any newcomer to this area should take advantage of the outstanding scenery of the Peak District; the Derbyshire Dales; the plethora of historic houses and architecture. This wealth of tradition, beauty and history will, hopefully, be matched by the choice of where to eat and stay – at all levels of price and quality.

The important national guide books are essential to many of the country's top rated restaurants. Indeed, in our own place, many people visiting for the first time are fully aware of our achievements and 'pedigree' before ever crossing the threshold. However, the need for a localised guide is often overlooked. I hope you will use this guide in the spirit in which it is intended – not as a league table of critiques, but as a useful addition to the more usual choice of guide books.

I wish you a relaxing stay in Derbyshire.

A. Bramley

Andrew Bramley,
Partner, The Old Vicarage, Ridgeway.

Tastes of DERBYSHIRE

The wealth of nature's bounty has invited visitors and settlers to Derbyshire and the Peak District since prehistoric times. The Peak District, which seduces modern tourists with its breathtaking scenery, was appreciated by Prehistoric Man for the shelter afforded by its caves, the sweet water of its cloughs, its wild game and its fruits and, as man's skills and power over the environment progressed, the minerals to be gleaned from the rocky sub-strata. Caves near Brassington, inhabited 5,000 years ago, provided a home for a lead miner and his family as recently as 1720. The Romans drew not only lead from the ground, but also therapeutic benefits from the warm spring waters at Buxton and Bakewell.

The Well at Buxton still attracts interest from locals and tourists alike and is celebrated in an annual well-dressing ceremony, at which the Well is decorated with scenes from the Bible made from thousands of petals pressed into clay. Modern visitors, though, are probably less inclined to drink the waters than to sample the beverages at local hostelries. It is comforting to discover that, as well as beers from the national breweries, which are well-represented in this area, so close to the nation's brewing capital, Burton-on-Trent, there are excel-

lent pub-brewed beers to be found. At Ingelby in The John Thompson Inn you can enjoy a full flavoured bitter and 'Lloyd's Skullcrusher' (which speaks for itself), and, at The Steamboat at Trent Lock, another range of pub brews. In days gone

by, a less potent Derbyshire beverage, Hopkos, flavoured with hops and ginger, was served to refresh harvesters.

Although dairying is the best known farming interest in Derbyshire, the county also boasts fertile arable land suitable for grain. Oats were an important crop in former times and feature in the county's culinary tradition. Cooked on a 'bakestone' made of gritstone, which was suspended over an open fire, or bought from the Oatcake Man and served to accompany the main dish, Oatcakes took the place of bread in many Derbyshire kitchens. Thor Cakes, from Wirksworth − biscuits

sweetened with treacle, spiced with ginger, and made even more tempting by a sprinkling of candied peel — are based on a mixture of oatmeal and wheat flour and offered as a sweet treat on November the fifth. Candied peel is also used in Derbyshire Parkin, Ashbourne Gingerbread and to decorate Gingerbread Men sold during Wakes Week.

Other recipes for teatime cakes abound in Derbyshire, but the area's most famous dessert must be Bakewell Pudding. Traditionally-made, it has a puff pastry, not, as is more usual today, a shortcrust, base liberally spread with strawberry or raspberry jam and filled with a creamy mixture of eggs, sugar and ground almonds. One recipe for Bakewell Pudding, given in an 1887 recipe book, included candied peel, layers of blackberry, apricot and strawberry jam, topped with cheesecake mixture, and must bear some similarity to the recipe misinterpreted by a cook at The Rutland Arms Hotel in Bakewell whose mistake lead to the production of the pudding which is now popular throughout England.

Bakewell, the Metropolis of the Peaks, nestles in the valley of the River Wye, which offers sport to the angler and rainbow and brown trout and grayling to diners in the dis-

trict. The sport of fishing the rivers of the Peak District was expounded in discourses in *The Compleat Angler,* published in 1676, by Izaak Walton and Charles Cotton, whose fishing lodge still stands overlooking the Dove. The area is rich in game, and venison, grouse, rabbit and pigeon all feature in traditional recipes. Venison and grouse are to be found on the Chatsworth Estate, but rabbit and pigeon have always been more freely available for Derbyshire's tables. Pigeon, for instance, was served dressed with grape sauce or mixed with other

meats in Medley Pie, whilst celery gives a distinctive flavour to a traditional Derbyshire rabbit casserole, which, with parsley dumplings, provides a substantial family meal. Celery is also used in a sauce to accompany roast chicken, stuffed with sage, onions and breadcrumbs, whilst Chesterfield Stew is a rich rabbit broth, fortified with a little red wine, in which rolls of beef, stuffed with a herby forcemeat, are cooked until deliciously tender.

Derbyshire is renowned for its dairy pastures. Most of the milk produced today is sold as liquid milk, but there is a tradition of cheese making in the county. Longford was the home of the first cheese factory in England and produced, of course, Derby Cheeses. Little Derby Cheese is still made

today, and is worth seeking out to combine with sage, tarragon, thyme, and marjoram to make Potted Herb Cheese, an unusual starter dish served with toast. Sage Derby is more widely available, the layers of sage producing not only a decorative appearance but imparting a characteristic flavour to the cheese. The tradition of cheese making also lives on in Hartington, where Nuttall and Company are best known for their Stilton. Dovedale is the only area in England, outside the Stilton region itself, where the cheese is legally allowed to be made. Of deservedly good reputation, Derbyshire-produced Stilton is particularly tasty when taken with Derbyshire Moorland Tarts — little crisp pastry tarts filled with sweetened currants and candied peel.

Hill sheep are to be found on the moorlands of the region. The Gritstone, a native breed, sports black and white markings on its face and grey fleece. Derbyshire Hot Pot — layers of mutton and onion — a succulent casserole, provided simple nourishment, as did mutton stew, which was flavoured, once more, with celery. Mushrooms have also been commercially grown in the county, a development of the gathering of wild mushrooms from fields in the autumn. Mushroom

Garden fruits used in pies and puddings include gooseberries and rhubarb; rhubarb fool, made with Derbyshire double cream and vanilla sugar, is a simple treat. Later in the year Pippin (apple) Pie is served, traditionally accompanied by a slice of cheese.

soup, made with flavourful field mushrooms, is a warming first course for an evening meal taken as the light fades into an early autumn night. Spring brings Shrove Tuesday, celebrated in Winster with a pancake race, run between the dark gritstone houses along the village street. Winster Pancakes are flavoured with grated orange peel and served with orange quarters. At Ashbourne the Up'ards (from the North of the Town) compete with the Down'ards (from the South end), on Shrove Tuesday and Ash Wednesday, in an ebullient football match, the goal posts being some three miles apart at either end of the town. Bilberry pie is a traditional summer pudding and, sweetened, enhanced with a little chopped mint and covered with sweet shortcrust pastry, bilberries epitomise the taste of a Derbyshire summer.

The observance of ancient customs and the enjoyment of not only the beauty of the landscape, but also the harvest it endows, make up threads in the tapestry of life in Derbyshire and the Peak District, drawing together Prehistoric Man and Modern Man. These days consumer choice demands international cuisine of restaurants, inns and hotels, but it is to be fervently hoped that dishes from Derbyshire's rich culinary history will continue to be found on the menus in the county and that you can experience for yourself the *Tastes of Derbyshire*.

Chef's Choice

In each of our regional **Where to Eat** guides, we ask an experienced chef, well respected in the area, to prepare one of his favourite menus:

Pasquale Barile

Pasquale Barile is head chef at The George Hotel, Hathersage. He comes from near Bari in southern Italy and trained firstly as a commis chef in various regions of his country. Arriving in Britain in 1983, he worked in an Italian restaurant in Hathersage before joining The George as commis chef. Now, as head chef, he leads a team of six, catering for diners and special functions.

"The idea of this menu is to combine the different recipes of various Continental kitchens (i.e. Italian, British and French) to create an interesting, appetising and colourful meal."

STARTER
Asparagus Consommé with Prosciutto

Care taken over the preparation and clarification of this delightful soup will be well worthwhile. To accompany, a good quality Manzanilla, which is actually a fino sherry, acquiring a salty character from being kept in bodegas at Sanlucar de Barrameda.

FISH COURSE
Poached Fillet of Sole stuffed with Smoked Haddock and Chives, glazed with a Sabayon Sauce

WINE
Gewürtztraminer AC Gustav Lorenz 1987
Clean, dry, yet perfumed and spicy. A good accompaniment to the haddock farce.

MAIN COURSE
Breast of Duckling with Green Peppercorns

WINE
Chateauneuf-du-Pape Domaine Font de Michel 1984
The duckling, presented in this way, carefully sliced, is pure pleasure, with a textural change being introduced by the 'soft' green peppercorns. This estate bottled wine is full bodied and fully complements the duckling.

PUDDING
Cream Caramel alla Marta

WINE
Monbazillac AC Château Monbazillac 1983
A golden Sauternes-style wine from Bergerac — rich, textured and intense, complementing the cream.

Introduction

This *Where to Eat* guide has been compiled to offer readers a good cross-section of eating places in the area. We do not only concentrate on the most expensive or the 'most highly rated' but endeavour to provide details of establishments which cater for all tastes, styles, budgets and occasions. Readers may discover restaurants (formal and informal), pubs, wine bars, coffee shops and tearooms and we thank proprietors and managers for providing the factual information.

We do not intend to compete with the established 'gourmet guides'. *Where to Eat* gives the facts – opening hours and average prices – combined with a brief description of the establishment. We do not use symbols or ratings. *Where to Eat* simply sets the scene and allows you to make the choice.

We state whether an establishment is open for lunch or dinner and prices quoted are for an à la carte three course meal or a table d'hôte menu, including service, as well as an indication of the lowest priced wine. However, whilst we believe these details are correct, it is suggested that readers check, when making a reservation, that prices and other facts quoted meet their requirements.

Two indexes are included at the back of the guide so that readers can easily pinpoint an establishment or a town or village. We always advise readers to use these indexes as, occasionally, late changes can result in establishments not appearing in a strictly logical sequence.

We hope that *Where to Eat* will provide you with the basis for many intimate dinners, special family occasions, successful business lunches or, perhaps, just an informal snack. A mention of this guide when you book may prove worthwhile. Let us know how things turned out. We are always pleased to hear from readers, be it praise, recommendations or criticism. Mark your envelopes for the attention of 'The Editor, Where to Eat Series'. Our address is:

Kingsclere Publications Ltd.
Highfield House, 2 Highfield Avenue,
Newbury, Berkshire RG14 5DS.

We look forward to hearing from you. Don't forget, *Where to Eat* guides are now available for nearly every region of Britain, Ireland and the Channel Islands, each freshly researched and revised every year. If you're planning a holiday contact us for the relevant guide. Details are to be found within this book.

Where to Eat
DERBYSHIRE & THE PEAK DISTRICT

DARLEYS ON THE RIVER

Darley Abbey Mills, Darley Abbey, Derby.
Tel: (0332) 364987

Hours:	*Open for lunch and dinner (last orders 10pm, 10.30pm Fri/Sat).*
Average Prices:	*A la Carte £16; Sun lunch £8.95.*
Wines:	*House wine £6 per bottle.*

With the background of a weir across the Derwent, the setting for Darleys could hardly be more pleasant. In this tastefully refurbished Grade II listed mill, pale pinks and greens blend restfully with natural beech woodwork. The restaurant has magnolia damask linen on its tables which sparkle with Italian crystal and silverware, all subtly lit by lamps. The sun terrace, used for meals outside in summer, offers lovely views across the Derwent and there is disabled access to all facilities. The cuisine is classic and includes a vegetarian banquet, a selection of pasta, rice, pastry and vegetable timbales, prepared daily. Other popular dishes include melon with forest fruits, and avocado and smoked chicken breast with lime mayonnaise on the starters list. Lamb cutlets reform and the unusual Orchard Blossom duck (with an apple and cider baste) may feature for main courses, or guests may discover how veal Covent Garden or supreme of chicken tropicana are prepared. Children welcome. Major credit cards accepted.

Darleys on the River

Darley Abbey Mills · Darley Abbey · Derby · Telephone 364987

RHODE ISLAND EXCHANGE

	1 Queen Street, Derby. Tel: (0332) 49008
Hours:	*Open for coffee, lunch, tea and dinner. Bar meals.*
Average Prices:	*A la Carte £11; snacks from £2.95.*
Wines:	*House wine £5.95 per bottle.*

Rhode Island Exchange is an American-themed bar and restaurant with 50's and 60's bric-a-brac lining the walls and lively background music to accompany its upbeat menu. There is a wide choice at each stage. For a starter or light snack, there are, for example, dips, loaded potato skins, peel 'n' eat prawns, calamari, tacos and shared dishes such as pick 'n' mix (a melange of chicken wings, crispy mushrooms, potato skins and bar-b-q ribs). Main courses continue in the same vein. There are Cajun steaks (from New Orleans with hot sauces); many burgers, such as the Boston burger with sautéed mushrooms and a red wine sauce; fish dishes such as Pacific seafood steak; Mexican dishes, such as spicy chicken enchilada and, for the health conscious, salads such as the Monterey salad (sliced chicken fillets, fresh pineapple, tomato and sweetcorn, all on top of a crispy salad mix). Finally, for dessert, try 'The Outrageous' (fudge brownie, topped with ice cream, chopped nuts, chocolate syrup and whipped cream) or some 'After in a Glass' such as 'Golden Cadillac' (Galliano and white crème de cacao with ice cream and whipped cream). Children's menu. Parties a speciality.

EXCHANGE
BAR · RESTAURANT

HAVE YOU HAD THE EXCHANGE EXPERIENCE?

DISCOVER A GREAT WAY OF LIFE. AMERICAN STYLE. OPEN FROM 12 NOON THROUGH TO 11.00pm. SEVEN DAYS A WEEK. COME IN ANYTIME AND HAVE A MEAL, A DRINK, A COFFEE, A SNACK. MOST OF ALL, HAVE FUN.

BALTIMORE EXCHANGE
CASTLE PARK MARINA, CASTLE BOULEVARD, NOTTINGHAM. TEL: 0602 411175
RHODE ISLAND EXCHANGE
1 QUEEN STREET,
DERBY DE1 3DJ. TEL: 0332 49008
WOODSTOCK EXCHANGE
95 ECCLESALL ROAD SOUTH,
SHEFFIELD. TEL: 0742 361573

EXCHANGE
BAR · RESTAURANT

GUIDO'S

Restaurant – Bar
25 Curzon Street
Derby DE1
Telephone (0332) 363739

GUIDO'S RESTAURANT-BAR

25 Curzon Street, Derby. Tel: (0332) 363739

Hours: *Open for coffee, lunch and dinner (last orders 10.30pm). Closed Sun/Mon evenings.*

Average Prices: *A la Carte £13.50; Table d'Hôte £5.95.*

Wines: *House wine £7.50 per litre carafe.*

Guido, the Italian owner of this popular restaurant in Derby city centre, is a Formula 3 racing driver with a love of good food and socialising. Here, on street level, there is a fresh pasta restaurant serving a range of authentic Italian specialities in a pleasant dining room with wicker furniture and peach fabrics. Upstairs, in the à la carte restaurant, shades of peach continue the theme, with subdued lighting, linen tablecloths, original pictures and silver service waiting. At the rear of the building is a lounge area, with comfortable couches designed by Guido himself and an intimate bar.

In true Italian tradition, the range of antipasti is appetising and tempting. Grilled grapefruit au fromage, scrambled eggs on toast with smoked salmon, deep-fried squid, avocado prawns and a fresh, daily-made soup with garlic bread are just some of the offerings, with the highlight of this course being the antipasti Armando for two people, which presents a selection of some of the starters already mentioned and other dishes.

Pasta, available as a starter or main course, is a house speciality. Linguine al tomare features shellfish in a wine and cream sauce with a hint of turmeric, whilst the pasta gialla takes its name from the sunny yellow pasta tubes it offers, contrasting with peppers and tomato.

Fish courses depend on the day's catch, which can be viewed by request. Poached fillet of salmon in a brandy and cream sauce, fillet of Dover sole pan-fried with sage and king prawns sautéed in garlic butter, white wine and parsley reveal the imagination here. The marmitta di pesce della casa, meanwhile, is a house concoction of seasonal fish in a light, tasty sauce, again for two people.

Steaks, chicken and veal also feature prominently, the steaks plainly grilled to your liking or presented with garlic, white wine and cream, crushed green peppercorns, red wine, brandy and cream or with pizzaiola sauce (tomatoes, onions, capers and olives). Pollo verde is chicken in a delicate leek and cream sauce, and vitello alla salvia is escalope of veal with sage and apple, moistened with cider.

A selection of fresh desserts completes the meal along with cappuccino or espresso coffee and a Continental cheese board. All major credit cards are welcome.

RISTORANTE MILANO

Lodge Lane, Derby. Tel: (0332) 41944

Hours: *Open for lunch and dinner (last orders 10.30pm).*

Average Prices: *A la Carte £13; Sun lunch £6.*

This Italian and Continental restaurant stands on the A6 inner ring road towards Matlock. In charge of the kitchen is top Midlands chef, Sidney Williams, and he prides himself on imaginative dishes, specialising in the unusual delicacy bottarga (a cured tuna fish roe). Other favourites include pasta with baby clams, calves' liver with onions in white wine and fillet steak with garlic and anchovies.

RISTORANTE MILANO
LODGE LANE
DERBY
TEL (0332) 41944

THE CAVENDISH ARMS

London Road, Shardlow. Tel: (0332) 792216

Hours: *Open for coffee, lunch and dinner (last orders 10pm).*
              Bar meals, except Sat evening.

Average Prices: *A la Carte £15; Sun lunch £6.95; snacks from £2.50.*

This popular free house is under the supervision of chef-proprietor Peter Dalton-Prior and offers traditional and internationally-inspired cuisine on all its menus. Devilled kidneys may be followed by grilled swordfish with Greek salad, for instance, although there are grills, steaks with a variety of sauces and house specials like pork Marsala, scampi thermidor and beef Wellington. Vegetarians catered for too.

THE CAVENDISH ARMS

LONDON ROAD, SHARDLOW

Tel: 0332 792216

BAY TREE RESTAURANT

4 Potter Street, Melbourne.
Tel (0332) 863358

Hours:	*Open for lunch and dinner (last orders 10pm). Closed Sun evening and Mon.*
Average Prices:	*A la Carte £18; Sun lunch £8.50 (5 courses).*
Wines:	*House wine £6.75 per bottle.*

The Bay Tree Restaurant, built in 1790, is situated in the heart of the small, historic town of Melbourne and has been restored to capture a friendly and intimate atmosphere, highlighted by a tasteful, country-style décor. The menu changes monthly, with an accent on local produce and fresh fish, featuring lobster, mussels and other shellfish. In the style of nouvelle cuisine, but with portions more plentiful and artistically presented, the choice of dish varies from a steak of Aberdeen Angus beef (marinated in soy sauce, topped with crisp, fried vegetables) to French breast of duckling (roasted and served with a sauce of orange curacao and fresh strawberries), or local pheasant (when in season). Although the menu provides more than adequate variety, requests for other dishes can be made. Vegetarians are catered for, with prior notice appreciated. Visa and Access cards welcomed.

Bay Tree Restaurant

4 POTTER STREET, MELBOURNE, DERBYSHIRE
Telephone: Derby (0332) 863358

Proprietor: V.A. Talbott
Proprietor Chef: R.W. Howell

17

THE BOARS HEAD HOTEL

Lichfield Road, Sudbury. Tel: (0283) 820344

Hours:	*Open for coffee, lunch and dinner (last orders 10pm carvery, 9.30pm restaurant). Bar meals.*
Average Prices:	*A la Carte £15; Table d'Hôte £8; Sun lunch £6.95; snacks from £2.25.*
Wines:	*House wine £5.25 per bottle.*

The Boar's Head is a country inn of character, dating back to the 17th century when it was a coaching inn on Lord Vernon's estate. He is reputed to have lost it whilst playing cards, although it is plain that its successive owners have looked after its reputation for cheerful hospitality and good food. Diners choose between an English Carvery, The Boar's Head à la carte restaurant and a bar serving lighter snacks. The carvery always offers at least two roasts and a selection of casseroles and other dishes. Bar snacks are popular, home-cooked and amply served. The à la carte restaurant, in turn, serves a changing menu and vegetarians are asked to consult when booking. A three course meal might be prawn, tuna and Waldorf salad, followed by fruits de mer in lobster sauce on a bed of rice, with one of the freshly made desserts to conclude. Half portions for children. Major credit cards accepted.

LICHFIELD ROAD

SUDBURY

DERBY DE6 56X

TEL: 0283 820344

THE BREADSALL PRIORY HOTEL

Moor Road, Morley. Tel: (0332) 832235

Hours:	*Open for coffee, lunch, tea and dinner (last orders 9.45pm). Bar meals.*
Average Prices:	*A la Carte £15; Table d'Hôte £15; Sun lunch £8.50; snacks from £3.*
Wines:	*House wine £7.95 per bottle.*

Breadsall Priory dates back to 1260, and the new extension to the hotel's already good facilities, will be completed, and completely in harmony with the old building, by June 1990 when the new restaurant opens to non-residents. The Monk's Bar with its log fire and real ales is already a pleasant place for a bar snack, whilst for a more substantial meal there is the Elizabethan Priory Restaurant with its leaded windows and comfortable, solid furniture. Relax over an à la carte selection of French and English dishes after a game of golf on the hotel's own course or a work out in the new leisure complex. Try asparagus hollandaise or coquille of prawns before rack of lamb or Dover sole. Vegetarians are offered savoury stuffed crêpes, for instance. A selection of desserts and cheeses precedes coffee and mints. Children's portions are available and there are access and facilities for disabled guests. Major credit cards welcomed. Four miles from Derby city centre.

BREADSALL PRIORY
HOTEL

MOOR ROAD

MORLEY

DERBY

DE7 6DL

TEL:
(0332) 832235

THE MIXING PLACE FARMHOUSE RESTAURANT

Dannah Farm, Bowmans Lane, Shottle, near Belper.
Tel: (077 389) 273

Hours: *Open dinner, except Mon/Tues, and lunch on Sun.*
Average Prices: A la Carte £15; Sun lunch £9.50.

Still a working farm, it would be difficult to find somewhere more rustic than this restaurant. Formerly a mixing place for animal feeds, it is now a mixing place of a different kind, a relaxing place for a sociable meal in farmhouse style. Quenelles of pike with hollandaise sauce and pheasant in cream and brandy are just two choices. Vegetarian dishes.

**THE MIXING PLACE
AT DANNAH FARM**

BOWMANS
LANE
•
SHOTTLE
(Nr. Belper)
•
DERBY
•
TEL
(077389) 273

THE ANCHOR INN

Chesterfield Road, Oakerthorpe, Alfreton.
Tel: (0773) 833575

Hours: *Open for lunch and dinner. Bar lunches.*
Average Prices: A la Carte £7; snacks from £1.95.

Out of 350 entries in the 1988 Pub Caterer of the Year competition, The Anchor Inn was selected as a finalist. The style is traditional, from the oak beams and horse brasses to the menu of popular pub fare. Steaks, pies, lasagne, chilli, salads, scampi, trout and more are offered, with a blackboard of daily specials and vegetarian options.

20

RACHELL'S RESTAURANT AND BARS

Hilcote Lane, Blackwell. Tel: (0773) 811248

Hours: *Open for lunch and dinner (last orders 10pm). Rest. closed Sun/Mon evenings. Bar meals, except Mon.*

Average Prices: *A la Carte £15; Table d'Hôte £8.50; snacks from 50p.*

Wines: *House wine £4.50 per carafe; 80p per glass.*

This modern, light and airy restaurant stands just five minutes from junction 28 of the M1. Attractively set out in pinks and soft greys, with modern pictures for added interest, it is personally supervised by proprietress Mrs Hoggard. Cuisine follows a traditional pattern, offering seafood platter, Scottish smoked salmon, chef's pâté maison and home-made soup of the day with croûtons amongst the starters. Main courses span chicken, duckling, pork and lamb, with a full selection of grills as a further alternative. Scampi, trout and fillet of sole cater for seafood lovers, whilst, for vegetarians, there are always dishes like broccoli and avocado quiche, vegetable crepes and the unusual Brazilian salad, featuring apple, celery and Brazil nuts. The scope of the menu is to be widened in the near future, with even greater choice in the offing. Occasional live vocalists add to the entertainment and dinner dances are another feature. Visa and Access cards are welcomed at this popular 45 seater restaurant and bar.

Rachell's

RESTAURANT AND BARS

HILCOTE LANE
HILCOTE
BLACKWELL
DERBYSHIRE
Tel: Ripley 811248

Turbutt Arms

Main Road, Stretton

0246 250096/250001

THE BOATHOUSE INN

Dale Road, Matlock. Tel: (0629) 583776

Hours: *Open for lunch and dinner (last orders 9pm, 9.30pm Sat). Bar meals, except Sun evenings in winter.*

Average Prices: A la Carte £6.50; snacks from £3.50; house wine £7.20.

A Grade II listed building, the 250-year-old Boathouse Inn is replete with brasses and a warming atmosphere. Visitors can dine in both the bar and restaurant areas, or in a family room. 'Borringe Pie', filled with beef in orange, is a creation of proprietress Viv Whitehurst; 'Lample Pie', meanwhile, features lamb with apples, and such innovation is balanced by favourites like Lancashire hot pot. Real ale.

THE ELIZABETHAN RESTAURANT

4 Crown Square, Bakewell Road, Matlock. Tel: (0629) 583533

Hours: *Open for morning coffee, lunch, and afternoon tea, 7 days. Dinner Fri/Sat in winter, Sun in summer.*

Average Prices: Lunch £2.95; Sun lunch £5.75; dinner from £5.

Built at the turn of the century, this cosy, bow-windowed restaurant is personally supervised by its owner Mr Faulkner. Traditional English farè is served, with fresh roasts daily. The many home-made dishes include savoury pancakes, steak and kidney pie, grills, steaks, fish, vegetarian meals and specials.

STRAND RESTAURANT

43 Dale Road, Matlock. Tel: (0629) 584444

Hours: *Open for lunch and dinner, Mon-Sat in summer; Tues-Sat in winter.*

Average Prices: Snacks and meals from £2; dinner from £7.50.

It used to be a draper's shop; today it is a 1920's style popular, informal restaurant, offering a varied menu of freshly prepared food, cooked with flair. Both lunch and evening menus are supplemented with a range of daily specials, dependent on the produce available at the vegetable, meat and fish markets. Wednesday is an Italian night, and one can dine to a live trad. jazz trio on Thursday evenings.

*Kingsclere Publications produces a varied list of publications in the **Where to Eat** series which cover areas as far apart as Scotland, The Channel Islands and Ireland.*

RIBER HALL

Matlock. Tel: (0629) 582795 Fax: (0629) 580475

Hours:	*Open for coffee, lunch, tea and dinner.*
Average Prices:	*A la Carte £23; Sun lunch £12.50.*
Wines:	*House wine £7.85 per bottle.*

On the borders of the Peak National Park, in the peaceful backwater of Riber Village, is Riber Hall, an Elizabethan manor house set in its own grounds with a delightful walled garden, orchard and conservatory. Eleven rooms, mostly with antique four poster beds and en suite bathrooms, provide the accommodation, whilst in the restaurant the French and English menu is always changing but the imagination and variety are constant. A selection for lunch might include hot Stilton soufflé with horseradish, followed by breast of chicken with a leek and chive cream, with gratin of strawberries in kirsch for dessert. The à la carte selection is characterized by spring lamb sautéed with baby vegetables and white wine, brill fillet with spring onion and saffron sauce and fillet of venison with pineapple, port wine and shallots. A dessert of armagnac ice cream with prunes in puff pastry and Kahlua sauce could complete the meal. There is also a vegetarian menu. Take junction 28 off the M1 and follow the A615, turning off at Tansley, to find this stately hotel. All major credit cards are welcome.

Antique four-poster beds - Whirlpool baths - Outstanding cuisine - Extensive wine list
Tennis court - Five Stately Homes and Peak National Park nearby
M1 (exit 28) 20 minutes

Telephone Matlock (0629) 582795

HODGKINSON'S HOTEL

150 South Parade, Matlock Bath. Tel: (0629) 582170

Hours:	*Open for coffee, tea and dinner. Bar meals.*
Average Prices:	*Table d'Hôte £17; bar snacks and meals from £3.*
Wines:	*House wine from £6.50 per bottle.*

Until the late 18th century, the main road between Matlock and Derby ran a mile to the east. The rocky barrier at Cromford was then dynamited and the road diverted through the small and quiet spa town of Matlock Bath. Hodgkinson's Hotel was the first coaching hotel to be built, known then as The Bath Hotel and bought in part, in 1830, by a Mr Job Hodgkinson from whom it gets its name. Built in front of a steep cliff, it contains as its cellars the old mineworkings reputed to go back to Roman times. Part of these mines and the Georgian wine vaults are now being converted to a new dining room for the hotel and will form a unique feature. The kitchen offers a menu of exciting seasonal dishes, such as mussels for starter, stuffed with a green pepper, garlic and parsley butter, then grilled. Main courses show equal imagination: fillet of beef stuffed with mushroom pâté and garlic, for instance. The tradition at Hodgkinson's Hotel of catering for the gentry has always been based on fine food and accommodation, standards that the present owners Malcolm Archer and Nigel Shelley are determined to continue. ETB four crowns.

SOUTH PARADE, MATLOCK BATH
DERBYSHIRE DE4 3NR
TELEPHONE: (0629) 582170

THE TAVERN AT TANSLEY

Tansley, Matlock. Tel: (0629) 57735

Hours: *Open for coffee, lunch, tea and dinner. Rest. closed Sun evening and Mon. Bar meals 7 days.*

Average Prices: *A la Carte £18; Table d'Hôte £12.50; snacks from 90p.*

French, traditional, vegetarian and bar meals, all are available at this 17th century, Grade II listed building which has been totally refurbished without detracting from its character and age. In the restaurant oysters Casino, lobster, scallops, grouse and venison add seasonal colour to the extensive à la carte selection. Fresh pies, pasta and more in the bar with its brasses and beams. Real ales.

The Tavern

———— at Tansley ————

Your hosts: Joan & Keith Colton

NOTTINGHAM ROAD, TANSLEY
MATLOCK

Telephone: (0629) 57735

TALL TREES COFFEE SHOP AND RESTAURANT

Oddford Lane, Two Dales, Matlock. Tel: (0629) 732932

Hours: *Open for coffee, lunch, tea and dinner.*

Average Prices: *A la Carte £5; snacks from £1; house wine £2.75.*

Tall Trees, on the A6 from Chatsworth to Matlock, is run by Anne Wallwork. An informal atmosphere welcomes visitors and Anne's home-cooking caters for all tastes, vegetarian included. Chicken, nutmeg and broccoli lasagne, smoky beef casserole and mushroom Stroganoff are favourites, with sticky pudding evenings attractive to those with a sweet tooth. Children welcome. Private parties by booking.

TALL TREES COFFEE
SHOP AND
RESTAURANT

Open Daily 10.00 - 5.30 p.m.
Morning Coffee - Lunches - Cream Teas

Oddford Lane, Two Dales, Matlock

Tel. Matlock 732932

CALLOW HALL COUNTRY HOUSE AND RESTAURANT

Mappleton Road, Ashbourne. Tel: (0335) 43403

Hours:	*Open for dinner, Tues-Sat, and lunch on Sun.*
Average Prices:	*A la Carte £20; Table d'Hôte £18; Sun lunch £9.*
Wines:	*House wine £5.10 per bottle.*

Home of David and Dorothy Spencer, Callow Hall stands half a mile from the centre of Ashbourne, surrounded by woodland and unspoilt countryside. A tree-lined approach leads into 44 acres of grounds and to the striking Victorian house itself. Within, the elegant dining room, drawing room and aperitif bar are furnished in period style, but it is David's Continental and English cuisine that continues to be the main attraction. Produce is local as far as possible, with beef reared on the estate and baking done on the premises to supply bread, pastries and puddings for the restaurant. The French menu reveals moules marinière and asparagus with lime butter amongst the starters from time to time, with thoughtfully prepared main courses like veal with wild mushrooms and beef en croûte to follow. A well stocked cellar ensures an excellent range of accompaniments. Spacious, comfortable accommodation is a further enhancement and there are facilities for disabled guests. All leading credit cards are accepted.

CALLOW HALL · ASHBOURNE (0335) 43403

BOWLING GREEN INN

2 North Avenue, Ashbourne. Tel: (0335) 45120

Hours: Open for dinner, except Mon/Tues, and bar meals, except Tues.

Average Prices: Table d'Hôte £12; snacks from £1.

A 17th century pub with open fires, the Bowling Green Inn revels in original beams and brasses. The intimate, bistro-style restaurant presents a combination of international and traditional dishes, ranging from deep-fried Camembert to lamb casserole, prawn and haddock creole, and scampi with crab and cream sauce. There is always a choice for vegetarians. Children catered for in the bar. Real ale.

YE OLDE VAULTS

Market Place, Ashbourne. Tel: (0335) 46127

Hours: Open for coffee, buffet lunch, tea and dinner (last orders 8.30pm). Bar meals evenings.

Average Prices: A la Carte £5.50; snacks from £2.

Ye Olde Vaults is a 200-year-old listed building of great character which has been conscientiously refurbished in a brasserie style with Spanish terracotta tiles and marble-topped tables. Draught Bass can accompany an English menu based on local produce. The lunchtime buffet of salads, hams and quiches is very popular, and there are always three hot dishes, with a range of tempting desserts to follow.

16/17 April — 87.50 67.50 incl bkfast

OLD BEAMS RESTAURANT WITH ROOMS

Waterhouses. Tel: (0538) 308254

Hours:	*Open for lunch and dinner (last orders 10pm). Closed Sun evening, and all day Mon.*
Average Prices:	*A la Carte £25; Table d'Hôte £10.25; Sun lunch £14.75 (5 courses).*
Wines:	*House wine £6.25 per half-bottle, £11.25 per bottle.*

The Old Beams, a coaching inn dating back to 1746, has been tastefully refurbished to present an attractive restaurant, as well as comfortable accommodation. Chef-patron Nigel Wallis and his wife, Ann, have developed a first class reputation for their classic French cuisine, enhanced by their own modern interpretations. Lamb filled with redcurrant mousseline and mint leaves, wrapped in pastry and baked, exemplifies the creativity of the kitchen. Wild duck with limes and watercress similarly shows flair, whilst tart of pigeon breast or fresh Dublin Bay prawns in pastry on a cream sauce reveal the inspiration behind the starters. Vegetarians are also looked after, and, once a month, adventurous guests can savour the mysteries of the surprise menu. Midway between Leek and Ashbourne, this beautiful restaurant stands about 35 minutes' drive from the M1 or M6, on the A523, in the rural setting of the Waterhouses Peak Park. All leading credit cards are welcome.

THE IZAAK WALTON HOTEL

Dovedale, near Ashbourne.
Tel: (033 529) 555 Fax: (033 529) 539

Hours: *Open for coffee, lunch, tea and dinner. Bar meals.*
Average Prices: *A la Carte £14; Table d'Hôte £12.50; snacks from £1.*
Wines: *House wine £7.10 per bottle; £9.34 per litre.*

This 17th century farmhouse played host to Izaak Walton when he fished in the nearby River Dove and collected material for his authoritative book *The Compleat Angler.* Far from a humble farmhouse these days, it is now a luxury hotel, set in its own grounds with magnificent vistas. The owner is the Duke of Rutland and his establishment has been honoured by four members of the Royal Family. The chef furnishes the Regency-style dining room with a combination of English and French dishes. Appetisers include cream of celery soup and asparagus and fig salad, before main courses like sugar-baked gammon with peaches and fillet of beef steak topped with blue cheese. Black cherry surprise is just one of the satisfying desserts. Children and vegetarians are looked after too and lighter meals are available in the bar. There is also a Buttery in the former dairy, where coffees, light lunches and traditional afternoon teas are served. Ample parking. Non-residents welcome. Major credit cards are welcomed.

The Izaak Walton Hotel

DOVEDALE NEAR ASHBOURNE DERBYSHIRE DE6 2AY
Tel: Thorpe Cloud (033 529) 555 (6 lines)
Telex: 378406 Izaak W. Fax: (033 529) 539
AA*** RAC*** Egon Ronay Recommended

EDWARDO'S BISTRO

110 Buxton Road, Whaley Bridge, Stockport.
Tel: (0663) 732002

Hours: *Open for lunch and dinner. Closed Mon.*
Average Prices: *A la Carte £10; Sun lunch £6.50 (4 courses).*

A building over 100 years old is the setting for the family-run Edwardo's Bistro. The cosmopolitan choice of dishes extends from lemon sole stuffed with minced scallops and crab meat, au gratin, to Edwardo's own curry and 'Kiss me Quack', half crispy roast duckling, coated with syrup, topped with red wine and cranberry sauce. Speciality evenings.

EDWARDO'S BISTRO

110 Buxton Road, Whaley Bridge, Stockport
Telephone: 0663 732002

THE PORTLAND HOTEL AND PARK RESTAURANT

32 St John's Road, Buxton. Tel: (0298) 22462

Hours: *Open for coffee, lunch, tea and dinner. Bar meals.*
Average Prices: *A la Carte £14; Sun lunch £7.50; snacks from £1.25.*

A family run, Victorian hotel, The Portland Hotel stands on the A53, opposite the Pavilion Gardens. Its elegant Park Restaurant (in the new, attractive, Victorian-style conservatory, with matching drapes, and furnishings) combines both French and English recipes on its menu, with dishes like scallops in Pernod, entrecôte Marchand de Vin and fillet of beef Stroganoff. Aubergine and mushroom lasagne for vegetarians.

AA ★ ★   **The Portland Hotel**   RAC ★ ★

32 St John's Road Buxton Derbyshire SK17 6XQ
Telephone (0298) **22462/71493**

ALEXANDRIA MEDITERRANEAN RESTAURANT

1-2 Lower Hardwick Street, Buxton. Tel: (0298) 72246

Hours: *Open for lunch, tea and dinner. Closed Mon lunch.*
Average Prices: *A la Carte £15, Sun lunch £7.75.*
Wines: *House wine £6.80 per bottle.*

The Alexandria Mediterranean Restaurant enjoys an exciting atmosphere, ideal for special occasions and group bookings. The décor summons up impressions of Greece, with palms and vines framing intimate alcoves for privacy, and there is a dance floor where guests can try dancing to live bouzouki, violin, accordion and mandolin music, with the friendly, fun help of the staff. Food is authentically Mediterranean in style and covers Turkish, Lebanese, Corsican, Egyptian, French, Spanish, Greek, Cypriot and Maltese dishes. An impressive choice of 28 starters begins the meal and the menu goes on to list a tempting choice of main courses, from which Billy 'Bulant', the belly dancing chef, recommends kleftico, the traditional Greek bandit's meal of leg of lamb, slowly baked with herbs, cloves and wine. He also specialises in Turkish kebabs of marinated meat with bay leaves, peppers and onions. Alternatively, there are no less than 34 other main dishes to choose from and an extensive wine list which includes Retsina. Children welcome. Leading credit cards accepted.

Alexandria
Mediterranean Restaurant

1-2 Lower Hardwick Street
Buxton
Derbyshire
SK17 6DQ
Tel: 0298 72246/72583

CHATTERS CONTINENTAL RESTAURANT AND WINE BAR

Eagle Parade, Market Place, Buxton. Tel: (0298) 71516

Hours:	*Open for coffee, lunch and dinner. Closed Sun lunch.*
Average Prices:	*A la Carte £9.50; snacks from £1.50.*
Wines:	*House wine £5.75 per bottle.*

Situated in the Market Place, in the beautiful Georgian spa town of Buxton, Chatters is one of a row of Victorian buildings. A recently renovated interior features open fireplaces, exposed brickwork walls, spiral staircases and ceiling fans. A soft glow from the coloured wall lights illuminates collected artwork, and pink and grey tablecloths help create a warm atmosphere. The friendly welcome from Anglo (Tony) and American (Janet) hosts extends to families, too, and the Continental menu reveals pizza and pasta temptations, and dishes such as saltimbocca alla romana (veal with Parma ham, sage and wine), and king prawns in garlic butter. There are several vegetarian dishes, and all dishes and sauces are prepared with fresh ingredients in Chatters' own kitchen. The wine list features excellent Italian labels, and the French wines include some medal-winning, organically-grown wines. Pre- and after-theatre meals are available for diners visiting Buxton's famed opera house. Most credit cards are accepted. Chatters also has a cellar wine bar, open evenings, and a functions room.

**CHATTERS
CONTINENTAL
RESTAURANT
& WINE BAR**

EAGLE PARADE

THE MARKET
PLACE

BUXTON

DERBYSHIRE

TEL:
(0298) 71516

COLD SPRINGS HOUSE HOTEL

Longhill, Manchester Road, Buxton. Tel: (0298) 72565
Hours: Open for dinner and Sun lunch. Closed Sun/Mon eves.
Average Prices: A la Carte £18; 12 wines under £9 per bottle.
Cold Springs House is a large Victorian mansion with delightful views.
The elegant restaurant serves freshly cooked, well presented French
food. The menu changes regularly but some specialities are soups, fresh
fish, casseroles, home-made puddings and ice creams. Over 60 wines
from nine countries. Major credit cards are welcomed. Take the Whaley
Bridge road out of Buxton.

ColdSprings House
H O T E L   R E S T A U R A N T
Open Tuesday to Saturday nights from 7.30 – last orders 9.30 –
also Sunday lunchtimes TELEPHONE: BUXTON (0298) 72565
Long Hill, Manchester Road, Buxton, Derbyshire SK17 6ST
The Restaurant accepts all major credit cards.

THE WHEATSHEAF HOTEL

Bridge Street, Bakewell. Tel: (0629) 812985
Hours: Open for lunch, tea and dinner.
Average Prices: A la Carte £7; Sun lunch £5.50; snacks from £2.80.
Traditional dishes combine with vegetarian recipes at this popular
Bakewell inn. Garlic Mediterranean prawns or chicken liver pâté could
lead on to chicken Kiev, home-made steak pie or vegetable lasagne or
chilli. Steaks and fish like haddock, plaice and scampi are also served,
with favourites for children. A wide selection of sweets concludes.
Traditional ales in the bar. Facilities for disabled guests.

MONSAL VIEW CAFE

Monsal Head, near Bakewell. Tel: (062 987) 346
Hours: Open for coffee, lunch and tea all week in summer.
Average Prices: Snacks 85p-£3.25; house wine 85p per glass.
This attractive café with polished wooden floors and pine furnishings,
decorated with dried flowers and warmed by an open fire, looks out
across the famous Monsal Dale and viaduct. Popular for a light
sandwich or a plateful of chilli with rice and salad, for example.
Vegetarians are looked after and afternoon tea, with scones and
home-made cake, is also served in this converted goat shed and cottage.

THE ASHFORD HOTEL AND RESTAURANT

1 Church Street, Ashford-in-the-Water, Bakewell.
Tel: (0629) 812725

Hours:	*Open for coffee, tea and dinner (last orders 9.45pm).*
Average Prices:	*A la Carte £15; Table d'Hôte £12; Sun lunch £6; snacks from £2.50.*
Wines:	*House wine £5.30 per carafe, £3.90 per bottle.*

The Ashford Hotel welcomes non-residents and offers full table d'hôte and à la carte selections, as well as special Sunday lunches and a tempting range of bar snacks. Bar meals vary from cidered rabbit pie, Derbyshire sausage and filled Yorkshire puddings to chicken cordon bleu and vegetarian spinach pasta, filled with Ricotta cheese and cooked in courgette, tomato and herb sauce. The table d'hôte menu offers 12 starters and 13 main dishes. Try hot potted shrimps, then pork casserole with brandy, cream and apricots, served with fresh vegetables and potatoes. A dessert from the trolley, or cheese and biscuits, precedes freshly ground coffee and sweetmeats. A la carte, diners will find a similarly wide choice, with fish delivered daily from Brixham. Proprietress, Susan Dawson, won the 1988 Gold Food Award by Bass North and William Stones, for her selection of meals. Visa and Access cards are welcomed. Two miles from Bakewell on the A6 towards Buxton.

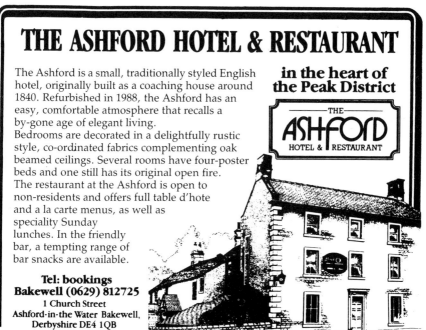

MONSAL HEAD HOTEL

Monsal Head, near Bakewell. Tel: (062 987) 250

Hours: *Open 11am-11pm, every day.*

Average Prices: *A la Carte £12; Table d'Hôte £9.75; bar meals, grills and snacks from £1.25.*

This authentically restored, four crown, Victorian residential hotel stands in the centre of the Peak District National Park. Family-run, it can be found two and a half miles north east of the market town of Bakewell, through the village of Ashford-in-the-Water, on the B6465, and, purpose built, it directly overlooks the beautiful Monsal Dale and surrounding countryside. The rear Stable Bar, with craft gallery above, specialises in at least five real ales, including Derbyshire Best Bitter and Weston's Scrumpy Cider, and serves bar meals, snacks, tea and coffee. A carvery operates lunchtimes and evenings in the Longstone Lounge Bar, providing bar meals and grills. The restaurant, in turn, is open from 7 to 9.30pm, offering a choice of no less than 18 main dishes from its table d'hôte and à la carte selections. Corn on the cob, vegetable samosa or chicken satay, to start, can precede recipes like veal cordon bleu, lamb Shrewsbury and vegetarian sweet and sour almonds for main course. Private parties, conferences and weddings catered for; Access and Visa cards accepted.

WARDLOW BULL'S HEAD

Wardlow, Tideswell, Buxton.
Tel: (0298) 871431

Hours: *Open for lunch at weekends and dinner each evening*
(last orders 9.30pm). Bar meals.

The Wardlow Bull's Head is situated in the heart of the Peak District
National Park on the B6465, an ancient Iron Age road through lovely
countryside leading up to spectacular views at Monsal Head. Meals at
the Wardlow Bull's Head are taken either in the genial bar, with its
gleaming copper tables and Wards traditional ales, or in a separate 60
cover restaurant, with oak beamed ceiling and friendly service, where
there is a special area for family dining. To start your meal there are
five options, including smoked salmon and chicken liver pâté. Main
courses always include a vegetarian dish (lasagne, for instance),
alongside steak and kidney pie with mushy peas, curried chicken,
seafood Mornay, cottage pie and a range of other meat and fish dishes,
grills and filled jacket potatoes. Side orders of chips, salad and garlic
bread are also available. The regional favourite Bakewell pudding
features among others to follow the main course. A blackboard gives
dishes of the day. An 18th century pub with lots of character.

The **WARDLOW BULL's HEAD**

Wardlow, Buxton · Tel: 0298 871431

37

THE THREE STAGS HEADS

Wardlow Mires. Tel: (0298) 872268
Hours: *Open for bar meals, 12.30-10.30pm.*
Average Prices: *Meals and snacks £1-£5.*
Wines: *House wine 90p per glass.*

As historic pubs go, The Three Stags Heads is in the top league. Its shape and its size are 17th century originals, and the flagstoning and oak beaming are genuine, not recent, additions. The site of the last public gibbeting, The Three Stags Heads nowadays lends itself to more convivial activities. Food-wise, the cook has interesting ideas and depending upon the produce available, turns out popular dishes like rabbit pie, casserole with cheese dumplings, sweet and sour chicken, steak and kidney pie and chick pea curry. Fresh herbs, vegetables and meat dominate proceedings, with local suppliers called upon. Profiteroles, boozy fresh fruit salad, hot bananas in rum, and apple and mince meat pie, reveal that the imagination does not end with the main courses. To the side of the inn are the pottery rooms (formerly cow barns) which produce the pottery used in the inn and also for sale to visitors. Ales, of course, are traditional. Once frequented by notorious highwayman, Black Harry, The Three Stags Heads is now called upon to play host to much gentler folk. Vegetarians catered for.

THREE STAGS HEADS · Wardlow Mires · Tel: 0298 872268

THE LAZY LANDLORD

Foolow, Eyam, near Sheffield. Tel: (0433) 30873
Hours: *Open for lunch and dinner.*
Average Prices: *A la Carte £9; snacks from £3.95.*

The traditional English fare at The Lazy Landlord is prepared by
Michael Holden, the far from lazy chef who used to work at Simpsons in
the Strand. His food is enjoyed in the heart of the beautiful Derbyshire
Peaks in this 200-year-old building which retains its original character.
Anything from sandwiches to egg, bacon and black pudding, or a full
three course à la carte meal is possible. Vegetarian and gluten-free
dishes too. Wards and Darley ales.

THE PEACOCK HOTEL

Rowsley, Matlock. Tel: (0629) 733518
Hours: *Open for coffee, lunch, tea and dinner.*
Average Prices: *Table d'Hôte £21; Sun lunch £9; snacks from £4.*

Once a manor house around which peacocks strode, this distinguished
hotel is a classified national monument. Over 150 years of hospitality is
brought to bear in the kitchen where pride in the preparation and
presentation of dishes is evident. Warm salad of duck and chicken
livers, followed by veal with basil, chick pea, red lentil, diced tomato and
white wine, are dishes which can only hint at the culinary flair
exhibited here. Lunchtime buffet, except Sunday.

The Peacock Hotel
Rowsley
Derbyshire
Tel: (0629) 733518

EAST LODGE COUNTRY HOUSE

Rowsley, Matlock. Tel: (0629) 734474

Hours:	*Open for coffee, lunch (bookings only), afternoon tea and dinner (last orders 8.30pm).*
Average Prices:	*Table d'Hôte £14.*
Wines:	*House wine £6.*

The East Lodge of Haddon Hall was sold in 1922 by the Duke of Rutland. Now it is an elegant hotel and restaurant with two dining rooms, both available for private functions. The larger is more formal, with an oak fireplace and furniture, old pictures and tables with linen cloths at which there is attentive service. Views extend over the ornamental lake and the large croquet lawn, for the use of guests. The smaller dining room, by contrast, is in the Laura Ashley cottage style. The menu is freshly prepared each day and is based on English traditions with Continental variations. The unusual baked stuffed squid may be discovered amongst the appetisers, to be followed by beef Wellington, roast duckling with orange and apricot sauce or escalopes of veal with lemon and tarragon sauce, perhaps. Vegetarians are not overlooked. A selection of home-made sweets and puddings is offered daily. Children are welcomed. There are 15 en suite bedrooms, including one on the ground floor with facilities for disabled guests.

EAST LODGE
COUNTRY HOUSE

Rowsley
Matlock
Derbyshire DE4 2EF
Telephone (0629) 734474

THE DEVONSHIRE ARMS

Beeley, Matlock. Tel: (0629) 733259

Hours: *Open for coffee in the bar; lunch, tea and dinner, except Sun (last orders 9.45pm).*

Average Prices: *Table d'Hôte £5; snacks from £2.50.*

Visitors to nearby Chatsworth House often pop into this lovely, authentic 18th century coaching inn for a meal or a snack. Theakston's and Wards real ales are served in a friendly atmosphere, along with a traditional menu with a wholefood bias. Try country casserole, chicken Kiev or perhaps spinach and walnut lasagne. Side orders of salad, chips or garlic bread complete the meal. Children welcome.

Beeley, Matlock, Derbyshire Telephone: 0629 733259

THE BARN HOUSE COFFEE SHOP

Church Terrace, Baslow. Tel: (024 688) 2293

Hours: *Open for coffee, lunch and tea. Closed Tues/Wed/Thurs, Oct-March.*

Average Prices: *A la Carte £6.50: Sun lunch £6.50.*

The Barn House is a converted 17th century barn which particularly welcomes walkers. The rustic interior has watercolours and old prints on the walls, traditional furniture with lace tablecloths and antique bric-a-brac for sale. Traditional and wholefood is served, including children's meals and vegetarian dishes. Soup or pâté to start, then steak and kidney pie, lasagne verdi or pork in cider is a popular choice,

Look out for . . .
Where to Eat
in North West England,
on sale now!

41

THE GEORGE HOTEL

Main Road, Hathersage. Tel: (0433) 50436

Hours: *Open for coffee, lunch and dinner. Bar meals, except Sat evening and Sun lunchtimes.*

Average Prices: A la Carte £15.75; Table d'Hôte £12.95; Sun lunch £7.95; bar meals from £1.20. House wine £5.95 per bottle.

Renowned for its character and comfort, The George Hotel dates from the 16th century and has been brought up to date without losing its original charm. The recent addition of the Morton Suite allows the hotel to take care of small conferences and private dining, whilst the Charlotte Restaurant can also accommodate receptions for up to 75 persons. It serves a combination of traditional and Continental dishes. Deep-fried cheese with Cumberland sauce or Chinese-style avocado feature amongst the starters, main courses ranging from escalope of pork in cream and Stilton sauce to 'Fillet in a Casket' (fillet steak in a light pastry casket, served with a sauce of home-made pâté, red wine and mushrooms). Apricot and walnut roulade continues the imagination into the dessert course. The George Bar, meanwhile, offers home-made deep fish pies, home-made soups, chilli con carne and more, with vegetarians not overlooked. Sausages, beans and chicken nugget type fare for children. Easily accessible from Sheffield, Leeds and Manchester, and a convenient base for tourists.

GEORGE HOTEL
Hathersage, Nr. Sheffield, Derbyshire (0433) 50436

THE NEW BATH HOTEL

Stretfield Road, Bradwell. Tel: (0433) 20431

Hours: *Open for bar meals. Trad. lunch on Sun.*

Average Prices: Snacks and meals £1.75-£4.50; house wine £3.95.

The New Bath Hotel is known locally as 'the pub with the view' because of its beautiful situation in the Peaks, off the B6049 between Castleton and Hathersage. There is accommodation in four family rooms, Marston's, Burton and Stones ales, and food which is freshly prepared each day. Traditional home-made pies are offered along with authentic Indian curries, vegetarian dishes and local salmon and steaks. Children welcome.

YE DERWENT HOTEL

Main Road, Bamford. Tel: (0433) 51395

Hours: *Open for coffee, lunch, tea and dinner.*

Average Prices: A la Carte £8.50; Sun lunch £5.50; snacks from £1.25.

At Ye Derwent Hotel, deep in Jane Eyre country, Angela and David Ryan pride themselves on their home-cooking and selection of traditional ales. Camembert puffs may precede home-made steak and kidney pie, tournedos Rossini or fresh local trout, with puddings like treacle tart and fruit pies to conclude. Club sandwiches, lasagne, scampi and other favourites in the bar. Vegetarian meals. Children also welcome.

Whilst we believe that all factual details are correct, we suggest that readers check, when making reservations, that prices and other facts quoted meet their requirements.

THE MARQUIS OF GRANBY HOTEL

Bamford, near Sheffield. Tel: (0433) 51206

Hours:	*Open for coffee, lunch and dinner. Rest. closed Sun evening and Mon. Bar meals, except Mon evening.*
Average Prices:	*A la Carte £10; Sun lunch £6.95; snacks from £2.50.*
Wines:	*House wine from £6.50 per carafe.*

On the outskirts of the village of Bamford stands this spacious, grand hotel. The Marquis of Granby reveals all the traits of being family-run, with an interior that is gracious and constantly updated without losing character. The small function room is unusually clad in walnut panelling from the luxury liner, The Olympic, whilst a small, elegant restaurant overlooks the lawns. Here the menu extends from the traditional to the international. The Dalesman's hors d'oeuvre couldn't be anything but Yorkshire pudding with onion gravy; New Orleans prawn cocktail, on the other hand, comprises Greenland prawns, smothered in tangy New Orleans sauce. Chicken Jamaican, for main course, is a dish of chicken and paprika; the plaice tropicana is garnished with banana and cashew nuts, and steak Nina features strips of fillet, tossed in yoghurt, almond liqueur, garlic and cream. An imaginative melon risotto thoughtfully caters for vegetarians. Children are welcome and there is ample choice in the bar, too.

THE RISING SUN HOTEL

Bamford, Sheffield. Tel: (0433) 51323

Hours: *Open for coffee, lunch, tea and dinner (last orders 9.30pm). Bar meals.*

Average Prices: *A la Carte £10.50; Table d'Hôte £5.75; snacks from £1.25.*

Wines: *House wine £7.25 per litre carafe.*

The Rising Sun Hotel is located on the A625 road, from Sheffield to Castleton, and offers a Tudor-style welcome through its beamed interior, open fires, an oak-panelled ballroom and dark wood furnishings. Diners can enjoy a meal either in the bar, which stocks real ales, the Oak Room Carvery with its three roasts and a chef's daily special, or the à la carte restaurant which seats 60. In the bar all the pub favourites are available, along with three vegetarian options and some oriental dishes. Again, in the restaurant there is an ample choice of popular dishes and some unusual items. Pork chops with apricot and spinach seasoning and Marsala sauce, steak Diane, scampi Pernod and chicken chasseur are just some of the popular dishes. Vegetarians are offered Stroganoff, biriani, lasagne or tagliatelle niçoise. Soup of the day, coupe Florida or perhaps Yorkshire pudding with onion gravy can begin, with a trolleyful of desserts to round off. Dinner dances and live music regularly feature.

THE RISING SUN HOTEL

CASTLETON ROAD, BAMFORD, SHEFFIELD S30 2AL

TELEPHONE: HOPE,VALLEY (0433) 51323

THE POACHER'S ARMS HOTEL

Castleton Road, Hope. Tel: (0433) 20380

Hours: *Open for coffee, lunch and dinner (last orders 9.30pm). Bar meals.*

Average Prices: *A la Carte £12.95; Table d'Hôte £10.50; Sun lunch £8.50; snacks from £1.10.*

Wines: *House wine £6.80 per bottle.*

The Poacher's Arms Hotel is a small, family run hotel half a mile out of Hope village on the road to Castleton. Guests can explore Castleton's famous limestone caverns where the local stone Blue John is found, or enjoy the outdoor pursuits of the Peaks. In accordance with its name, the hotel is filled with pictures of game and stuffed animals, and the general atmosphere is homely and comfortable. The chef concentrates on providing country-style cooking for both the bar and restaurant. Snacks as light and inexpensive as a mug of home-made Poacher's soup with a home-made bread roll, or local black pudding in a cider and apple sauce, served with cranberries and home-made bread, are always available, whilst, in the restaurant, dishes on the four course menu extend from starters like savoury choux bun, stuffed with a hot, creamy chicken and bacon filling, to main courses such as Hawaiian lamb cutlets and rabbit casserole. Vegetarians have eight dishes to choose from, including noodle and ratatouille bake. All credit cards accepted.

THE POACHERS ARMS

CASTLETON ROAD · HOPE

DERBYSHIRE
TELEPHONE · (0433) 20380

THE OLD VICARAGE

Ridgeway Moor, Ridgeway, near Sheffield.
Tel: (0742) 475814

Hours: *Open for dinner, Tues-Sat, and Sun lunch.*
Average Prices: *Set prices from £19.50; Sun lunch £12.*
Wines: *From £7 per bottle.*

The county's Restaurant of the Year for two consecutive years now, this 1840's country house stands at the head of the delightful Moss Valley. A winding gravel drive leads to the main house and the acres of landscaped grounds, originally laid out by a celebrated horticulturist and explorer. They contain many fine specimens, like the 70ft. cedars of Lebanon, imported from the Middle East as seedlings. The interiors are all one would expect from a house of this calibre. Fine antiques, paintings, Persian rugs and log fires provide a relaxing setting for the nationally acclaimed cooking of chef Tessa Bramley. The food changes very much with the seasons, and is based primarily on Mrs Bramley's extensive kitchen gardens. Popular dishes include wild rabbit casseroled with foie gras, pot-roasted partridge or turbot with a langoustine sauce. The cooking is influenced by good regional dishes; try the chocolate pudding with fudge sauce and custard. The wine list is considered to be among the best in England, strong in classic areas, with many offerings under £10.

THE OLD VICARAGE

RIDGEWAY MOOR, RIDGEWAY, DERBYSHIRE
Nr. SHEFFIELD S12 3XW   TELEPHONE (0742) 475814

UPLANDS MANOR RESTAURANT AT PARK HALL HOTEL

Spinkhill, Sheffield. Tel: (0246) 434897

Hours: *Open for coffee, lunch, tea and dinner (last orders 9.45pm). Rest. closed Sun evening.*

Average Prices: *A la Carte £15.50; Table d'Hôte £12.95; Sun lunch £8.50. House wine £6.95 per litre carafe.*

Park Hall Hotel is a 16th century manor house set in eight and a half acres of delightful countryside, only three minutes from junction 30 of the M1, off the A616 near Eckington. The rooms are oak-panelled with open fires and plush carpets, and the restaurant is decorated in toning pinks and beiges, to complement the silver service. From every window the beauty of the Derbyshire countryside can be savoured, and, on Saturdays, a pianist adds to the atmosphere. The owners, Mr and Mrs Clark (a cordon bleu cook), have created a varied French menu to match the elegance of the setting. Try scallops à la crème, then lemon sole baked with shallots, thyme, Chablis and cream, or medallions of beef pepperonata with peppers, onions, white wine, oregano and tomatoes. Mr and Mrs Clark do their best to provide any dish requested on booking. Regular Continental evenings and dinner dances are featured. All credit cards are accepted.

Park Hall Hotel ★ ★ ★

Park Hall Hotel and Restaurant is pleasantly situated close to the Peak District. The hotel offers excellent accommodation full of olde worlde charm and roaring log fires. The restaurant offers a la carte and table d'hote, and Sunday lunches. Business meetings, breakfast meetings, weddings, anniversaries and parties catered for.

and "Uplands Manor" Restaurant
Spinkhill, Sheffield S31 9YD
Tel. (0246) 434897/435807

THE MANOR HOTEL AND RESTAURANT

High Street, Dronfield, near Sheffield.
Tel: (0246) 413971

Hours:	*Open for coffee, lunch, tea and dinner. Bar meals.*
Average Prices:	*A la Carte £12; Table d'Hôte £11.95; Sun lunch £6.95.*
Wines:	*House wine £6.75 per bottle.*

As its name suggests, The Manor Hotel was indeed a manor house, right up to the 18th century, when it was altered to make four cottages. Links with the past have certainly not been severed, as the characterful décor reveals and as the ghost of Lady Catherine, one-time owner of the manor, insists on proving. The restaurant today is a comfortable country style room, allowing 65 covers and welcoming residents and non-residents. Banqueting, conference and private party facilities are also available. The menu covers French and English recipes and has a healthy eating section and vegetarian dishes. Starters are popular and offer avocado prawn Mornay and deep-fried breadcrumbed clams, served with lemon and salad, amongst other dishes. Main courses are varied, offering baked trout with capers, guinea fowl with honey and armagnac, entrecôte bordelaise and tagliatelle with celery and almonds. Banana or peach flambé, perhaps, and then one of the many liqueurs or ports can complete the meal. Leading credit cards welcomed.

Manor Hotel

AND RESTAURANT

"For the Finer Things, with Time, in a picturesque setting"

HIGH STREET, DRONFIELD
NR. SHEFFIELD ☎ (0246) 413971

GOFF'S RESTAURANT AT LANGWITH MILL HOUSE

Langwith Road, Nether Langwith, Mansfield.
Tel: (0623) 744538

Hours: *Open for lunch and dinner. Closed Sun and Mon eves.*
Average Prices: *A la Carte £18; lunch £7.25; Table d'Hôte £13.50.*
Wines: *House wine £3.95 per carafe.*

Mr and Mrs Goff have been running this popular restaurant for five years, so successfully that a move to larger premises, just two and a half miles away, became essential. You find them on the A632 road, from Chesterfield to Newark, in a lovely 18th century, three-storey house. The décor is in keeping with the period, and charming views of the garden, with its intriguing 18th century textile mill, are afforded by the large Georgian windows. French and modern British cuisine is the attraction, with fresh fish well to the fore. Sirloin of beef with a charlotte of mushroom and courgette and a tomato and fresh basil sauce, may be balanced on the menu by magret of duck with a fresh lime butter sauce with Chartreuse liqueur, or haunch of venison served sliced on a cake of red cabbage with raisins and a whisky butter sauce, and there is always a freshly prepared vegetarian dish each day. For the even more adventurous, an innovation is the 'Menu Mystique', where guests can leave the choice of dishes to the chef (Tuesday to Friday).

LANGWITH ROAD
NETHER LANGWITH
TEL: (0623) 744538

MR C's CHANDELIER BAR AND RESTAURANT

69-71 Low Pavement, Chesterfield. Tel: (0246) 207070
Hours: *Open for coffee, lunch and dinner. Closed Sun.*
Average Prices: *A la Carte £12-£15; snacks from 95p.*

Mr C's is right in the heart of Chesterfield. Full of atmosphere, character and interesting features, it serves a varied menu of freshly cooked produce, with a display of fresh fish. Menus change regularly, ranging from avocado prawns to chateaubriand, and even fish and chips and vegetarian dishes. Adventurous bar lunches. Speciality evenings, including 4 July. Wines and champagnes from around the world.

69-71 LOW PAVEMENT
CHESTERFIELD
DERBYSHIRE
TEL: (0246) 207070

BEJERANO'S AT THE CHESTERFIELD HOTEL

Malkin Street, Chesterfield. Tel: (0246) 271141
Hours: *Open for lunch and dinner (last orders 10pm). Bar meals.*
Average Prices: *A la Carte £12; Table d'Hôte £10.95; Sun lunch £6.50.*

Bejerano's 20's-style feel, complete with pianist and weird and wonderful cocktails, makes a novel setting for a special occasion. Menus change weekly around a traditional theme. Smoked trout with raspberry and dill, or Chesterfield soup, then turkey escalope with blue cheese, or Derbyshire grill, followed by tropical Pavlova, are example dishes. Cakes made to order for celebrations. Most cards taken.

BEJERANO'S

RESTAURANT · LOUNGE & COCKTAIL BARS
The Chesterfield Hotel, Malkin Street, Chesterfield. Telephone: (0246) 271141

Enjoy a superb meal in an elegant hotel!
Bejerano's restaurant is renowned for the excellence of its cuisine, prepared by our Chef in both traditional and adventurous styles, and at prices you can afford.
Our splendid A la Carte menu and ever changing Table D'Hote will delight your palate.
Our Restaurant manager will be delighted to welcome you.

STONEY'S BAR AND RESTAURANT

Heath Road, Holmewood, Chesterfield.
Tel: (0246) 854609

Hours: *Open for coffee, lunch, tea and dinner. Bar meals.*

Average Prices: *A la Carte £14.50; Table d'Hôte £6.75; Sun lunch £7.95; snacks from 75p.*

Wines: *House wine £3.95 per bottle.*

Stoney's Bar and Restaurant is only a mile from junction 29 of the M1 and, as such, is a convenient spot to find accommodation (eight rooms) and a restaurant and bar serving a range of wholesome meals and snacks at sensible prices. A blue and pink décor, enhanced by comfortable chesterfields and velvet upholstered chairs, sets the scene. Dining in the 36 seater restaurant is offered à la carte or from a table d'hôte menu, which offers a choice of soup, seafood brioche, smoked mackerel, melon or fruit juice to start and a roast of the day, game pie, steak, trout, beef salad or vegetable pancake roll to follow, at the all-inclusive price with dessert or cheese and coffee. More extravagant dishes, à la carte, include queen scallops in Grand Marnier sauce and chicken breast with whisky, cream and prawns. At the other end of the scale, the bar menu offers chip butties, but also favourites like chicken, ham and mushroom pie, and scampi. Stoney's also welcomes parties and conferences. Visa cards accepted.

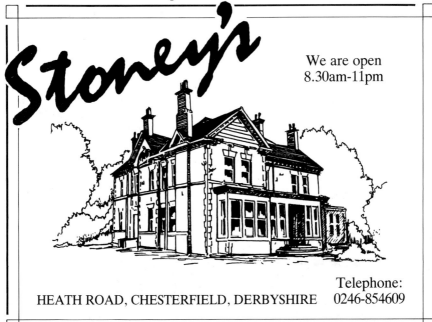

We are open
8.30am-11pm

HEATH ROAD, CHESTERFIELD, DERBYSHIRE

Telephone:
0246-854609

THE WHITE HART INN

Matlock Road, Walton, Chesterfield. Tel: (0246) 566392
Hours: Open for bar meals, except Sun evenings.
Average Prices: A la Carte £6; Sun lunch £5.95; snacks from £1.

The homely bars of The White Hart Inn convert into dining rooms every lunchtime and evening, so popular is the pub food. Real ale or a full wine list accompanies and children are welcome at lunchtime. Anything from a snack to a full meal or vegetarian feast is possible: devilled chicken, then trout almondine or the unusual pork Mombasa. Partner George Lee was formerly manager of award-winning Gravetye Manor.

The White Hart Inn

*Matlock Road, Walton,
Chesterfield S42 7LG*

Tel.: (0246) 566392

BLUE BELL INN

Station Road, North Wingfield, Chesterfield.
Tel: (0246) 850076
Hours: Open for coffee, lunch and dinner. Bar meals.
Average Prices: A la Carte £10; Table d'Hôte £7.95; Sun lunch £6.25.

The Blue Bell Inn was once a Chantry House belonging to the local church. Built in 1488, it now enjoys Grade II status as a listed building, with a splendid old stone fireplace and Tudor oak beams. French and English dishes are served: Camembert fritters, followed by tournedos Rossini, for example. Saturdays see a dinner and disco, and barbecues.

BLUE BELL INN

NORTH
WINGFIELD
CHESTERFIELD (0246) 850076

The
Shoulder of
Mutton Hotel

AT HARDSTOFT

HARDSTOFT, PILSLEY
Nr CHESTERFIELD
DERBYSHIRE
S45 8AF
Tel. Chesterfield (0246) 850276

THE SHOULDER OF MUTTON HOTEL

Hardstoft, Pilsley, Chesterfield. Tel: (0246) 850276

Hours: *Open for lunch and dinner (last orders 10pm). Bar meals lunchtimes and evenings.*

Average Prices: *A la Carte £18; bar snacks from £1.50.*

Originally a farm with a public house, which belonged to the Chatsworth Estate, The Shoulder of Mutton is now a free house which has been refurbished to create a four star hotel.

Owned and run by Ian and Caroline Whittock, it benefits from their notable experience in the trade. Ian was formerly executive chef at The Waldorf and the Park Lane Hotel in London, and Caroline also worked at The Waldorf, as well as at the Café Royal. They have introduced new talent to the kitchen team in the form of chef John Sweeney and it is his menu of French and other international dishes which is proving a major attraction.

The hors d'oeuvre selection features such appetisers as cream of onion soup, laced with cider and apple croûtons, and a ragoût of fish, set in a puff pastry case on a creamy dill flavoured sauce. Alternatively, a delicate salmon terrine on a bed of champagne sauce or a winter salad of rare leaves with warm wild mushrooms and Parma ham might appeal.

Fillet of beef with a shallot soufflé on a Madeira sauce is one of the highlights of the main courses, competing for attention with veal fillet with spinach, wrapped in filo pastry with a mild Roquefort sauce; breast of chicken filled with mango, with a mild curry sauce, and trimmed lamb cutlet in a creamy sorrel sauce. Seafood lovers can indulge themselves on turbot, lightly steamed and filled with wild mushrooms on a watercress sauce, or perhaps Dover sole fillets, glazed with herb breadcrumbs, on a bed of leeks with a white wine sauce dotted with truffles. Game, poultry and pork also feature prominently and vegetarians are looked after too, with all dishes presented in the modern style.

Panelled in dark red, with subdued lighting, the dining room has a low ceiling, which adds atmosphere, and alcoves to conjure intimacy. The conservatory, meanwhile, overlooks the gardens and offers a different, carvery style of dining. Five course dinner dances are an added attraction. The bar, as well as having Ruddles County on draught, presents a menu of snacks and meals.

Children are welcome at The Shoulder of Mutton and all leading credit cards are accepted.

THE LOCKOFORD INN

Lockoford Lane, Tapton. Tel: (0246) 275844

Hours:	*Open for coffee, tea and dinner, Tues-Sat (last orders 9.45pm). Bar meals, except Sun evening.*
Average Prices:	*A la Carte £8.50; Sun lunch £6.50; snacks from £1.*
Wines:	*House wine £4.25 per bottle.*

The Lockoford Inn, found off Tapton bypass, close to the new Sainsbury, is a reminder of the area's rural past, for it is 300-years-old and was once a farmhouse. Now owned by Mr and Mrs Navin, antique collectors, it is attractively furnished and displays an interesting collection of old clocks, which is the inspiration behind the name of the Chimes Restaurant. The cooking centres on traditional English fare, offering dishes like home-made steak pie, country casserole and a grill for large appetites, consisting of steak, pork chop, lamb chop, gammon, liver, kidney, sausage and chips, all available at the bar. Dinner, à la carte, takes much of its style from the Continent, with frogs' legs amongst the starters and steak au poivre as a main course. Fillet of pork sautéed in butter and presented with a mushroom sauce and duck à l'orange are two further possibilities, with dishes such as vegetable moussaka and lasagne always available for vegetarians. Facilities for disabled guests.

The Lockoford Inn

FREEHOUSE & RESTAURANT
Lockoford Lane, Tapton, Chesterfield
Telephone: (0246) 275844

To assist readers in making the sometimes confusing choice from the menu, we have listed some of the most popular dishes from restaurants featured in *Where to Eat* up and down the country, together with a brief, general explanation of each item. Of course, this can never be a comprehensive listing — regional trends result in variation in the preparation of each dish, and there's no accounting for the flair and versatility of the chef — but we hope it offers readers a useful guideline to those enigmatic menu items.

STARTERS

Foie gras .... duck or goose liver, often made into pâté
Gazpacho .... a chilled Spanish soup of onion, tomato, pepper and cucumber
Gravad lax .... raw salmon marinated in dill, pepper, salt and sugar
Guacamole ...... a creamy paste of avocado flavoured with coriander and garlic
Hummus .... a tangy paste of crushed chick peas flavoured with garlic and lemon
Meze .... a variety of spiced Greek hors d'oeuvre
Moules marinière .... mussels in a sauce of white wine and onions
Samosa .... small pastry parcels of spiced meat or vegetables
Satay .... small skewers of grilled meat served with a spicy peanut dip
Taramasalata .... a creamy, pink paste of fish roe
Tzatziki .... yoghurt with cucumber and garlic
Vichyssoise .... a thick, creamy leek and potato soup, served cold

FISH

Bouillabaisse .... chunky fish stew from the south of France

Coquilles St Jacques .... scallops
Lobster Newburg .... with cream, stock and, sometimes, sherry
Lobster thermidor .... served in the shell with a cream and mustard sauce, glazed in the oven
Sole Walewska .... a rich dish of poached fish in a Mornay sauce with lobster
Sole bonne femme .... cooked with stock, dry white wine, parsley and butter
Sole véronique .... poached in a wine sauce with grapes
Trout meunière ...... floured, fried and topped with butter, parsley and lemon

MAIN COURSES

Beef Stroganoff .... strips of fillet steak sautéed and served in a sauce of wine and cream
Beef Wellington .... beef in a pastry crust
Boeuf Bourguignon .... steak braised in a red wine sauce with onions, bacon and mushrooms
Chateaubriand .... thick slice of very tender fillet steak
Chicken à la King .... pieces of chicken in a creamy sauce
Chicken Kiev .... crumbed breast filled with herb butter, often garlic
Chicken Marengo .... with tomato, white wine and garlic
Chicken Maryland ... fried and served with bacon, corn fritters and fried banana
Osso buco .... knuckle of veal cooked with white wine, tomato and onion
Pork Normandy .... with cider, cream and calvados
Ris de veau .... calves' sweetbreads
Saltimbocca alla romana ...... veal topped with ham, cooked with sage and white wine

Steak au poivre .... steak in a pepper and wine sauce
Steak bordelaise .... steak in a red wine sauce with bone marrow
Steak Diane .... steak in a peppered, creamy sauce
Steak tartare .... raw, minced steak served with egg yolk
Tournedos Rossini .... fillet steak on a croûton, topped with foie gras and truffles
Wiener Schnitzel .... escalope of veal, breadcrumbed and fried

SAUCES

Aioli .... strong garlic mayonnaise
Anglaise .... thick white sauce of stock mixed with egg yolks, lemon and pepper
Arrabbiata .... tomatoes, garlic and hot peppers
Béarnaise .... thick sauce of egg yolks, vinegar, shallots, white wine and butter
Carbonara .... bacon, egg and Parmesan cheese
Chasseur .... mushrooms, tomatoes, shallots and white wine
Dijonnaise .... cold sauce of eggs and mustard, similar to mayonnaise
Hollandaise .... egg yolks and clarified butter
Mornay .... creamy sauce of milk and egg yolks flavoured with Gruyère cheese
Pesto .... basil, marjoram, parsley, garlic, oil and Parmesan cheese
Pizzaiola .... tomatoes, herbs, garlic and pepper
Provençale .... tomato, garlic, onion and white wine
Reform ..... pepper and white wine with boiled egg whites, gherkins and mushrooms
Rémoulade ...... mayonnaise with mustard, capers, gherkins and herbs, served cold

DESSERTS

Banoffi pie .... with toffee and banana
Bavarois .... cold custard with whipped cream and, usually, fruit
Crème brûlée .... caramel-topped, rich vanilla flavoured cream
Crêpes Suzette ...... pancakes flavoured with orange or tangerine liqueur
Parfait .... chilled dessert with fresh cream
Pavé .... square shaped light sponge
Pavlova .... meringue-based fruit dessert
Sabayon/zabaglione .... whisked egg yolks, wine and sugar
Syllabub .... whipped cream, wine and sherry
Zuccotto .... a dome of liqueur-soaked sponge filled with fruit and cream
Zuppa inglese .... an Italian trifle

CULINARY ITEMS

Coulis .... a thin purée of cooked vegetables or fruit
Croustade .... a case of pastry, bread or baked potato which can be filled
Devilled .... seasoned and spicy, often with mustard or cayenne
Dim-sum .... various Chinese savoury pastries and dumplings
Duxelles .... stuffing of chopped mushrooms and shallots
En croûte .... in a pastry or bread case
Farce .... a delicate stuffing
Feuilleté .... filled slice of puff pastry
Florentine .... containing spinach
Goujons .... thin strips of fish
Julienne .... cut into thin slices
Magret .... a cut from the breast of a duck
Mille-feuille .... thin layers of filled puff pastry
Quenelles .... spiced fish or meat balls
Roulade .... stuffed and rolled
Sauté .... to brown in oil
Tournedos .... small slice of thick fillet

Index

ALPHABETICAL INDEX TO ESTABLISHMENTS

ALPHABETICAL INDEX TO TOWNS AND VILLAGES

WIN A GOURMET DINNER FOR TWO
AT A TOP LOCAL RESTAURANT!
VOTE FOR THE
Where to Eat
RESTAURANT OF THE YEAR!

We are looking for Derbyshire and The Peak District's Restaurant of the Year, to be featured in the next edition of **Where to Eat.**

During the compilation of the next edition, we shall be asking the region's caterers for their choice of best eating place. However, we would like you, the readers — people who regularly dine out — to take part as well.

A form is provided below for you to tell us what you consider to be the best eating place in the area. It could be an establishment featured in this guide, or a recommendation of your own. And it doesn't matter whether you nominate a formal restaurant, a country inn, a town pub, a wine bar/bistro or even a coffee shop or tearoom.

In addition, the prize of a gourmet meal for two will be awarded to the reader who gives us the best reason for eating out rather than eating in (in not more than 20 words), irrespective of his/her choice of restaurant.

My choice for Restaurant of the Year is

_____

at _____

I prefer to eat out rather than eat in because

_____

_____

Name _____

Address _____

Please send your votes to:

Restaurant of the Year
Where to Eat in Derbyshire
Kingsclere Publications Ltd.,
2 Highfield Avenue,
Newbury, Berkshire, RG14 5DS

Closing Date: 1 October 1990

ORDER FORM

To:
KINGSCLERE PUBLICATIONS LTD.
Highfield House, 2 Highfield Avenue, Newbury, Berkshire RG14 5DS

Please send me

____ copies of *WHERE TO EAT in BERKSHIRE* @ £1.95 £ ____
____ copies of *WHERE TO EAT in BRISTOL, BATH & AVON* @ £2.50 £ ____
____ copies of *WHERE TO EAT in CHANNEL ISLANDS* @ £1.50 £ ____
____ copies of *WHERE TO EAT in CORNWALL* @ £1.95 £ ____
____ copies of *WHERE TO EAT in CUMBRIA & THE LAKE DISTRICT* @ £1.95 £ ____
____ copies of *WHERE TO EAT in DERBYSHIRE & THE PEAK DISTRICT* @ £1.95 £ ____
____ copies of *WHERE TO EAT in DORSET* @ £2.50 £ ____
____ copies of *WHERE TO EAT in EAST ANGLIA* @ £2.95 £ ____
____ copies of *WHERE TO EAT in EAST MIDLANDS* @ £1.95 £ ____
____ copies of *WHERE TO EAT in GLOS & THE COTSWOLDS* @ £1.95 £ ____
____ copies of *WHERE TO EAT in HAMPSHIRE* @ £1.95 £ ____
____ copies of *WHERE TO EAT in HERTS, BUCKS & BEDS* @ £1.95 £ ____
____ copies of *WHERE TO EAT in IRELAND* @ £2.95 £ ____
____ copies of *WHERE TO EAT in KENT* @ £2.95 £ ____
____ copies of *WHERE TO EAT in NORTH EAST ENGLAND* @ £1.95 £ ____
____ copies of *WHERE TO EAT in NORTH WEST ENGLAND* @ £1.95 £ ____
____ copies of *WHERE TO EAT in OXFORD & OXFORDSHIRE* @ £1.95 £ ____
____ copies of *WHERE TO EAT in SCOTLAND* @ £1.95 £ ____
____ copies of *WHERE TO EAT in SOMERSET* @ £1.95 £ ____
____ copies of *WHERE TO EAT in SURREY* @ £1.95 £ ____
____ copies of *WHERE TO EAT in SUSSEX* @ £2.95 £ ____
____ copies of *WHERE TO EAT in WALES* @ £2.95 £ ____
____ copies of *WHERE TO EAT in WILTSHIRE* @ £1.95 £ ____
____ copies of *WHERE TO EAT in YORKS & HUMBERSIDE* @ £1.95 £ ____

p&p at £0.50 (single copy), £1 (2-5 copies), £2 (6 copies) £ ____

GRAND TOTAL £ ____

Name ....

Address ....

....

Post code .... Cheque enclosed for £............................

Your help in answering the following would be appreciated:

(1) Did you buy this guide at a SHOP □   TOURIST OFFICE □   GARAGE □   OTHER □

(2) Are any of your favourite eating places *not* listed in this guide? If so, could you please supply names

and locations ....

....

....